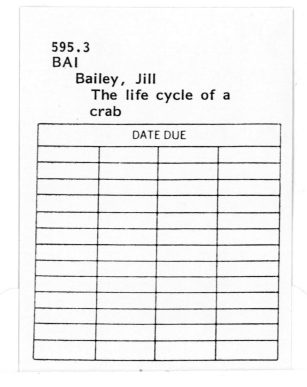

595.3
BAI
   Bailey, Jill
      The life cycle of a
   crab

DATE DUE			

The Life Cycle of a

CRAB

Jill Bailey

Illustrated by
Jackie Harland

Reading Consultant:
Diana Bentley

The Bookwright Press
New York · 1990

Life Cycles

First published in the
United States in 1990 by
The Bookwright Press
387 Park Avenue South
New York, NY 10016

First published in 1989 by
Wayland (Publishers) Limited
61 Western Road, Hove
East Sussex, BN3 1JD, England

© Copyright 1989 Wayland (Publishers) Limited

Library of Congress Cataloging-in-Publication Data
Bailey, Jill.
    The life cycle of a crab / by Jill Bailey.
        p.   cm.—(Life cycles)
    Bibliography: p.
    Includes index.
    Summary: Describes the physical characteristics,
habitat, food, and reproductive cycle of the crab.
    ISBN 0–531–18317–3
    1. Crabs—Life cycle—Juvenile literature. (1. Crabs.)
I. Title.   II. Series.
QL444.M33B333   1990
595.3′842—dc20   89–34735
                                                      CIP
                                                      AC
Typeset in the UK by DP Press Limited, Sevenoaks, Kent
Printed by Casterman S.A., Belgium

Notes for parents and teachers
Each title in this series has been specially written and
designed as a first natural history book for young readers.
For less able readers there are introductory captions,
while the more detailed text explains each illustration.

Contents

All the words that are
in **bold** are explained in
the glossary on page 31.

A crab's body is covered with a hard shell.

A crab has five pairs of legs, but the front legs are the largest. They end in a pair of big **pincers**. Behind the legs is a small, wide, curled-up tail. This is called the **abdomen** and is found under the crab's shell. The crab's eyes are on stalks. A crab can watch for enemies even when it is buried in the sand.

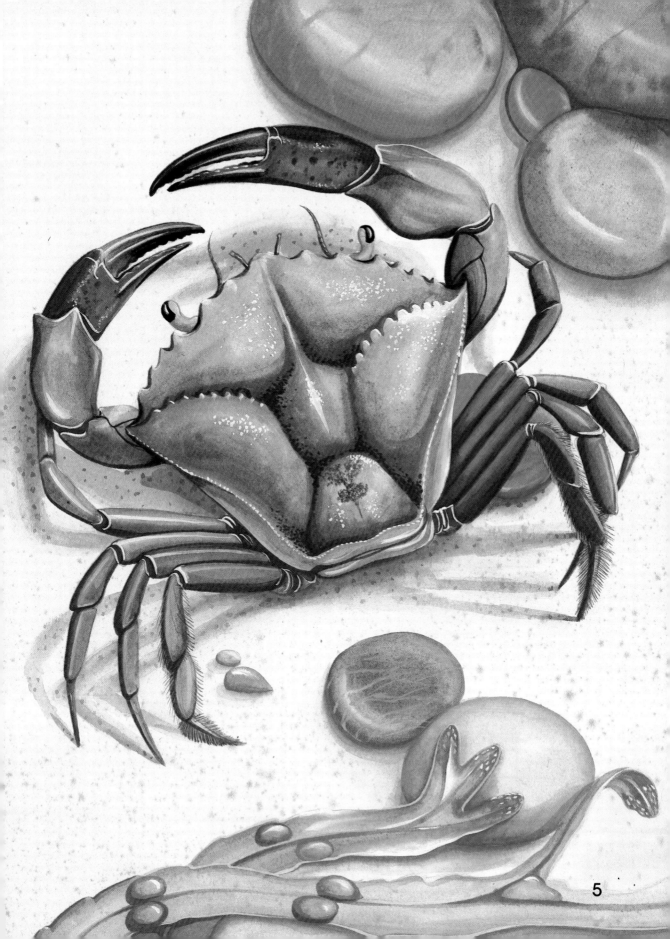

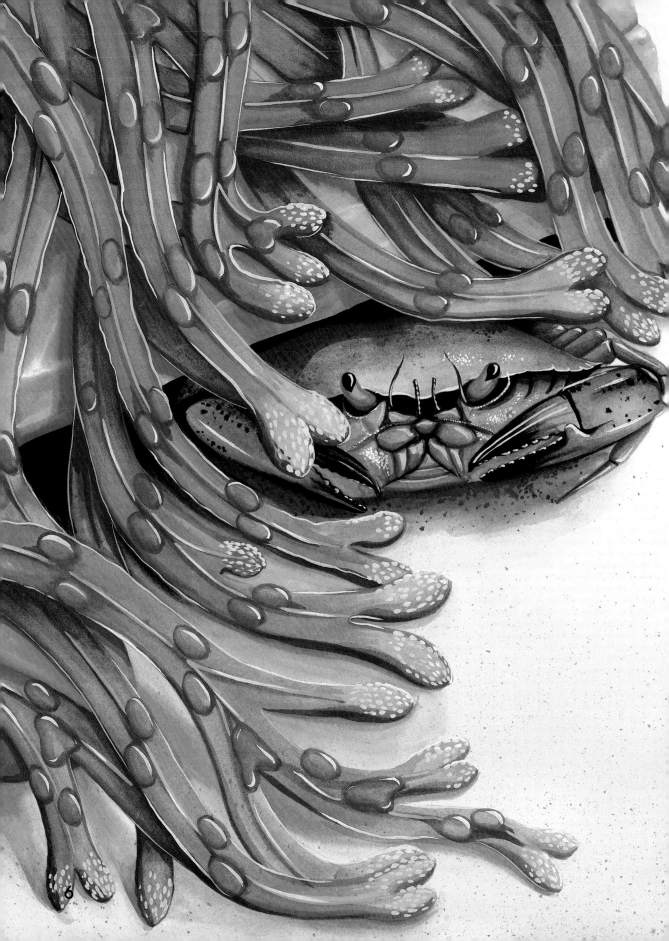

Crabs hide during the day.

Crabs live on the seashore. They come out to feed at night when their enemies, such as seagulls, cannot see them. Crabs search for food when the tide is in. During the daytime crabs hide in rockpools, under seaweed, or buried in the sand.

Crabs feed on fish or on seaweed.

Young crabs dig up worms with their pincers. Larger crabs can attack shrimps and other **shellfish**. Crabs also feed on dead animals, such as fish and jellyfish, that have been washed up by the sea. The crab has a hard, horny pair of jaws, called **mandibles**. It uses these for cutting up its food. Tiny mouthparts that look like little moving legs put the food into the crab's mouth.

A crab can run and swim.

A crab usually walks sideways on tiptoe. If it is disturbed it will run quickly to the nearest rocks. Here it can squeeze its flattened body into a crack where its enemies cannot reach it. Crabs can also swim by using their feet as paddles.

In spring the male crab finds a female.

When the male crab finds a female, he waves his legs to invite her to join him. Then he seizes her firmly around the middle. He may have to guard her for several weeks to prevent other males from taking her away. He is waiting for her to shed her shell.

The male and female crabs **mate**.

When the female crab has shed her shell, her body is very soft and ready for mating. The male turns her around to face him. Then he places some packets of a special liquid, called **sperm**, in two little hollows between her back legs. The sperm will make it possible for her eggs to grow.

The female crab produces her eggs.

A few weeks or perhaps even months after mating, the female crab produces thousands of tiny eggs. She fixes them to the stiff bristles on her abdomen, and carries them around tucked under her tail until they **hatch**.

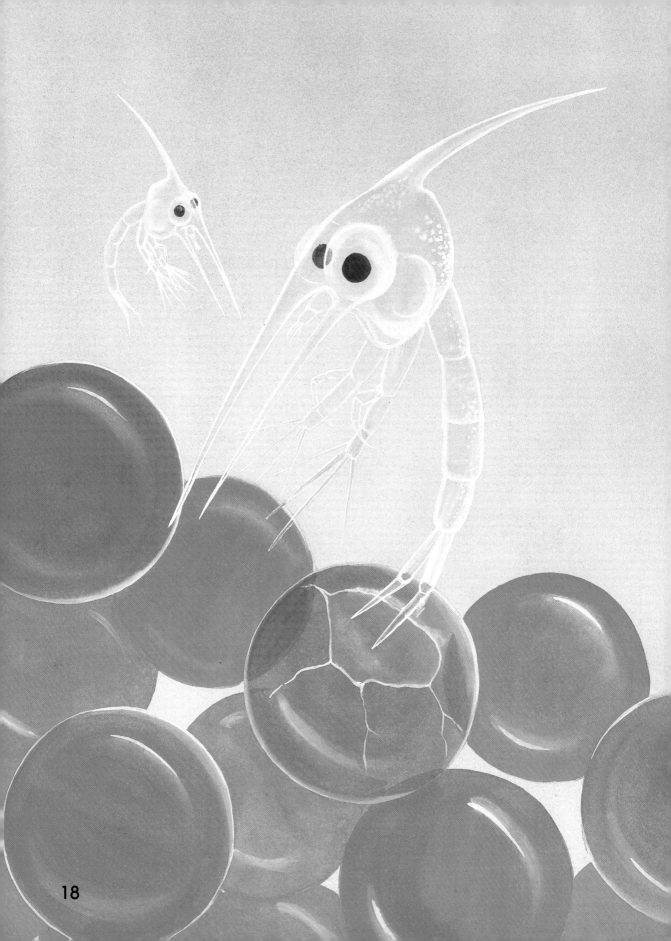

The eggs hatch into **larvae**.

The crab's larvae are strange little creatures. They are transparent – you can see right through them. They have large eyes and very long spines. The mother crab uncurls her tail and lets the larvae swim away. These larvae are called **zoea larvae**.

The zoea larvae swim and feed in the sea.

Each larva has legs that are covered with stiff bristles. These act like paddles for swimming. The zoea larva feeds on even tinier floating plants and animals. It traps its food between the bristles on its legs.

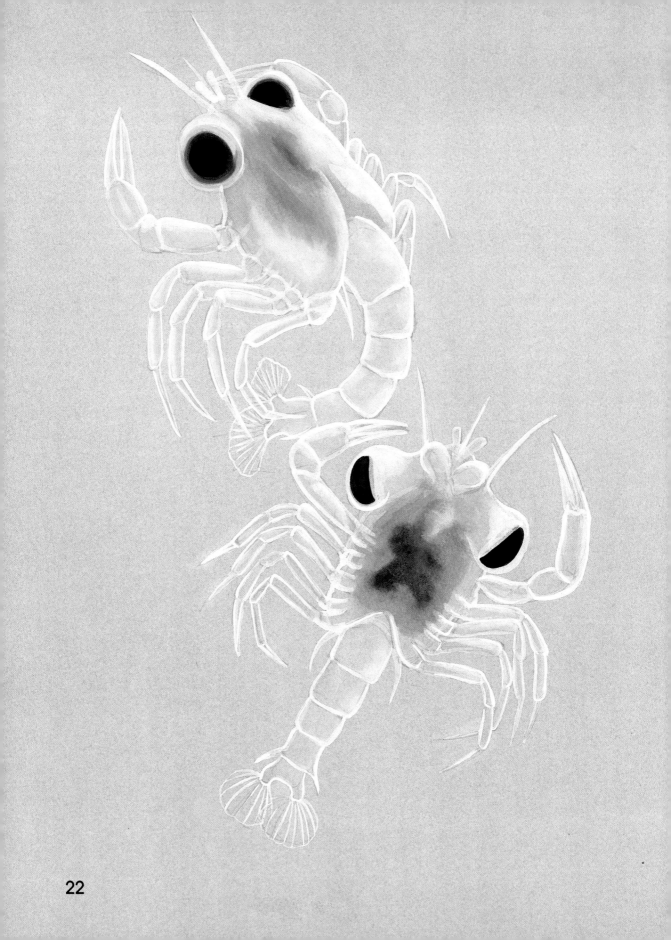

The larvae change into baby crabs.

After a while the larvae change shape. They are now called **megalopa larvae**. They look more like crabs, but their tails are not yet curled under their bodies. When a megalopa larva grows too heavy to float, it sinks down to the sand and mud at the bottom of the ocean and starts to live like a crab.

The baby crabs grow into bigger crabs.

The shell cannot stretch as the crab grows, so from time to time the crab must grow a new and larger shell. This is called **molting**. This is a most dangerous time, because the crab's body is very soft while the new shell is growing. The crab hides under rocks and seaweed until its new shell is hard.

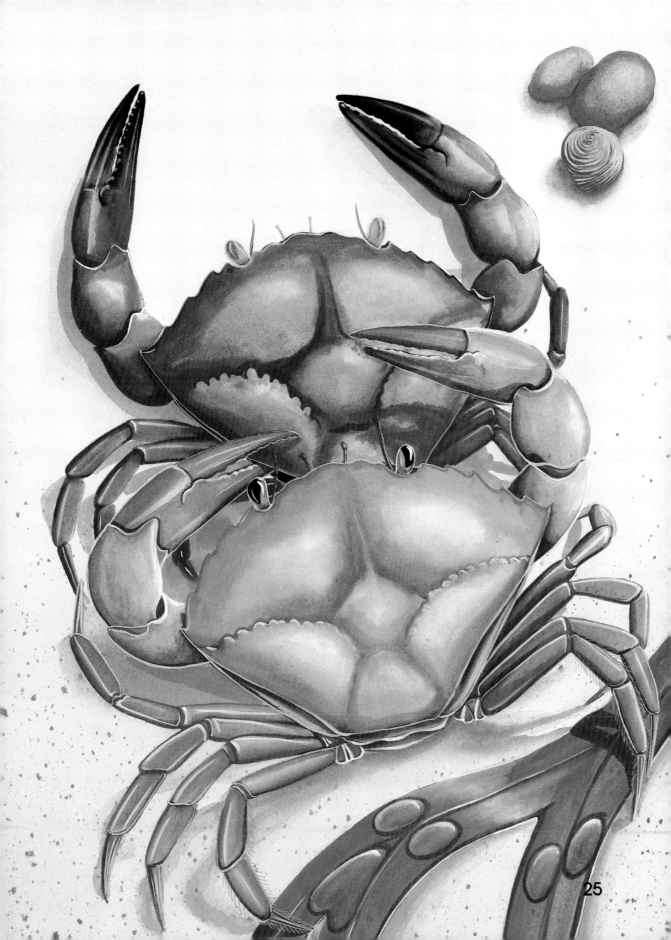

Crabs have enemies.

Crabs are often eaten by seagulls and other birds. Even in the ocean, fish, lobsters, octopuses and squid all find crabs a tasty meal. If a crab is attacked, it may grab its enemy with a pincer, then run off, leaving the claw behind. The crab can grow another claw the next time it molts. When the crab has molted for the last time, it is ready to look for a mate.

Looking at crabs.

It is easy to find crabs in rockpools. Look under the seaweed or rocks. Be careful – a large crab can give your fingers a painful nip. Gently use a stick to investigate. You can fish for crabs by hanging some food, such as pieces of meat or orange peel, on a piece of string. Carefully lift the crab out of the water as it clings to the food with its pincers. If you want to watch a crab, put it in a small rockpool where it will be covered by the tide later.

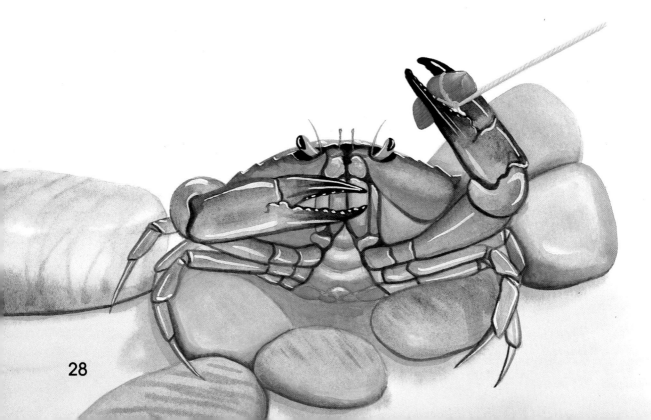

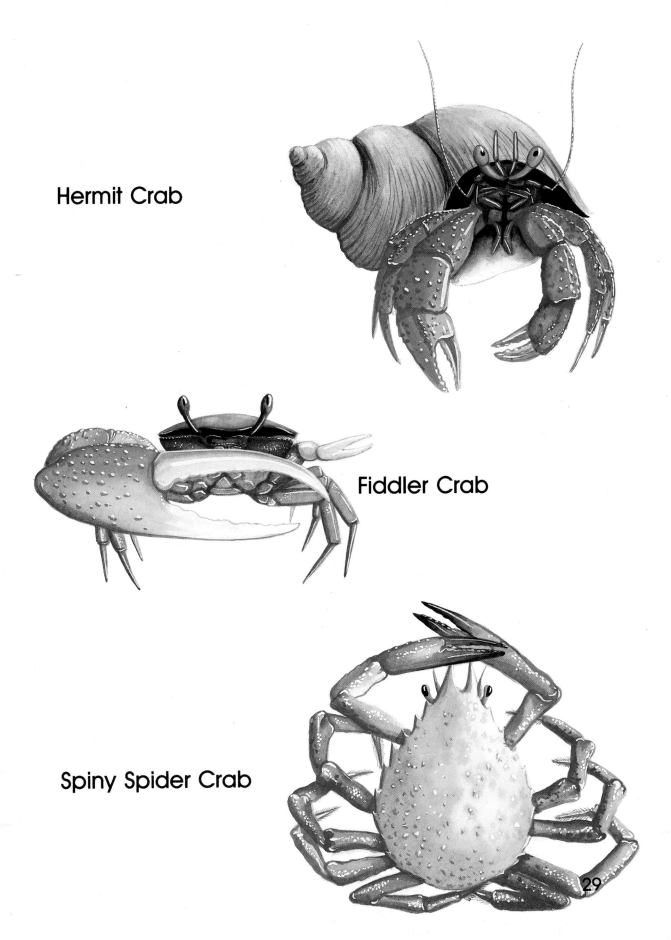

Hermit Crab

Fiddler Crab

Spiny Spider Crab

29

The life cycle of a crab.

How many stages of the life cycle of a crab can you remember?

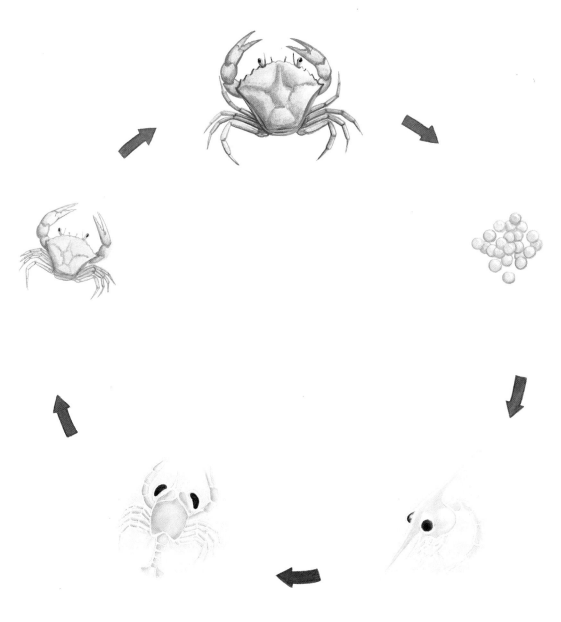

Glossary

Abdomen The tail end of a crab. The abdomen is usually curled under the crab's body.

Hatch To break out of an egg.

Larvae Baby animals, such as baby crabs and insects, that have a different shape from their parents.

Mandibles Horny jaws.

Mate To join together as male and female to produce young.

Megalopa larva The zoea larva changes into a megalopa larva before becoming a crab. The megalopa is like a tiny crab, except that its abdomen is not curled under its body.

Molting This is what happens when the crab gets too big for its shell. The old shell comes off and a new, larger shell grows.

Pincers The claws of a crab.

Shellfish Animals that live in the ocean and are covered with a shell. A crab is a shellfish. So are lobsters and oysters.

Sperm A liquid from the male crab. It mixes with the female crab's eggs. If this does not happen, the eggs will not grow.

Zoea larvae The kind of larvae that hatch from the crab's eggs. They have long spines.

Finding out more

Here are some books to read to find out more about crabs.

Discovering Saltwater Fish by Alwyne Wheeler
    Bookwright, 1988
Discovering Crabs and Lobsters by Jill Bailey
    Bookwright, 1987
Life in the Sea by Philip Steele
    Warwick, 1986

Index